DATE DUE

APR 22 1997			
NOV 04 1998			
OC 24 '02			
NO 15 '02			
FE 24 '03			
MY 05 '03			
NO 25 '03			
AP 27 '04			
MR 30 '07			
FEB 21 '08			
OCT 06 '09			

PRINTED IN U S A

Military Aircraft Library
Land-Based Fighters

0225
F195

Military Aircraft Library
Land-Based Fighters

DR. DAVID BAKER

Rourke Enterprises, Inc.
Vero Beach, FL 32964

LAND-BASED FIGHTERS

Typical of modern high performance combat planes, two General Dynamics F-16 fighters patrol the Hawaiian coast. Many foreign allies in Europe and around the world have bought fighters of this type from the United States to equip their own air defense units.

Library of Congress Cataloging-in-Publication Data

Baker, David, 1944-
Land-based fighters.
(Military aircraft library)
Includes index.
Summary: Describes the history and design of land-based fighter planes, their uses in combat, and the training necessary to fly them.
1. Fighter planes—United States—Juvenile literature. [1. Fighter planes. 2. Airplanes, Military] I. Title. II. Series: Baker, David, 1944- . Military planes.
UG1242.F5B36 1987 358.4'3'0973 87-14142
ISBN 0-86592-351-5

CONTENTS

How Fighters Evolved

One of the most important jobs in any conflict is to win control of the skies over enemy ground, over friendly ground, and over sea forces. If the enemy can use his own planes against defending or attacking troops, he may slow down the assault and cause many more casualties. Or he may reverse the advantage and gain ground. For these reasons, planes designed to gain control of the skies over a battlefield are especially important. At sea, naval fighters help protect ships under attack from enemy planes. They are also used to guard attacking aircraft operating from carriers.

Land-based fighters have evolved over many years. They were one of the first types of aircraft developed for use in war. Yet it was not until twelve years after the Wright brothers first flew in 1903 that planes were specifically designed to fight in the air. When the First World War broke out in Europe in 1914, fighting planes did not exist. Within a year guns had been fitted to small aircraft used to spy on the enemy. By 1918, when the war was over, whole

The Republic Thunderbolt was one of the more robust fighters to come out of World War II, seen here with early air-to-air missiles.

One of the first United States Air Force jet fighters, the F-84, was developed in fighter, fighter-bomber and reconnaissance versions.

The Thunderchief seen here was one of the first United States supersonic fighters.

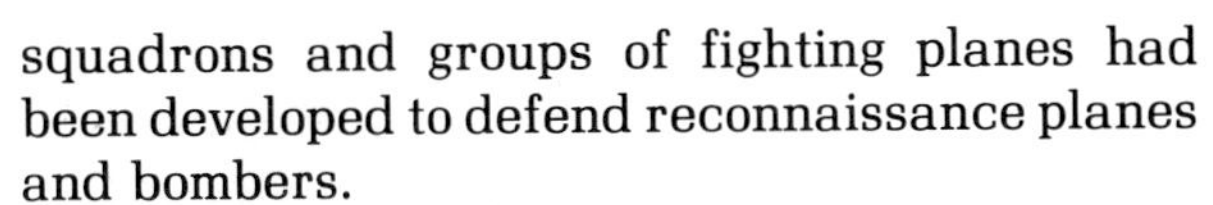

squadrons and groups of fighting planes had been developed to defend reconnaissance planes and bombers.

Probably the most important development of all was the concept of fighters attacking fighters. It pushed engineers and gun designers into new areas of work, which resulted in the creation of fighting machines used against each other. It created needs that produced more powerful engines and aircraft that could survive strenuous aerobatics. At the end of the First World War, fighters could reach speeds of more than 140 MPH. Some could reach a height of

Convair's F-106 Delta Dart could exceed Mach 2 and became a strong arm of the Tactical Air Command.

8,000 feet in just six minutes compared with a best time of twenty-three minutes in 1915.

By the end of the Second World War (1939-45), fighters could fly at around 400 MPH and reach a height of 20,000 feet in just ten minutes. Further developments were limited by the internal combustion engine and the propeller fitted to all combat planes before jets. Jets are really like rocket motors. To burn the fuel, however, they take in air through an intake, usually just ahead of the engine or in the plane's nose, whereas rocket motors carry their oxygen in special tanks. Germany and Britain developed the world's first jets toward the end of the Second World War, but the United States built the first production jet to see major combat duty.

Called the F-86 Sabre, this swept-wing fighter entered service in 1949 and proved itself superior to Russian-built Mig jets during the Korean War (1950-53). It had most of the design features that make up a typical jet fighter and helped the U.S. Air Force (USAF) develop the high speed combat tactics that would be used to train the new jet aircraft pilots. The Sabre had a top speed of 679 MPH and could reach a height of 12,150 feet in one minute! When it first appeared, the Sabre was almost twice as fast as most of the existing propeller-driven fighters and could climb six times more quickly.

Today front-line fighters are much more powerful than that first Sabre. A combat plane like the McDonnell Douglas F-15 can fly well over twice as fast as the Sabre and climb at 40,000 feet a minute. Today's fighter planes are specially designed for different tasks. Some fly high and very fast, while others fly more slowly but maneuver better at low speeds. Some have fixed wings, like the F-15, while others have wings attached to hinge backwards in flight. Called *variable-geometry* wings because they change their shape in the air, they enable these planes to perform many different roles. These include air defense, interception, attack, dog-fighting and even escort duties. Whatever its job, the modern fighter is a complicated piece of technology that brings together the skills of many different designers and engineers.

Four generations of famous fighter. From bottom to top, the T-38 trainer, the F-104 Starfighter, the F-4 Phantom and the F-15 Eagle supersonic interceptor.

Designed For Combat

Like the F-111 seen here, some planes have wings that can sweep back for high speed flight.

The way a plane is designed depends on the mission it is going to fly. If it has to fly both high and low at different times, it will probably have a variable geometry wing. This wing design allows the pilot to sweep the wings back for *supersonic*, high-altitude flying or forward for subsonic flight very close to the ground. Flying fast, close to the ground, causes buffeting on a wing designed primarily to give good handling at high altitude. Buffeting can place too much stress on the airframe and cause fatigue in the metal or the structure.

With a variable geometry wing, a fighter can take off from rough strips in shorter distances, using the wings in the normal position, sweeping them back to make a high speed, high altitude,

The robust and exceptionally strong F-15 Eagle is built for all-weather, high-speed, combat duty under all conditions. It also has the capability to operate as a fighter-bomber. Note the orange propellant tanks in the wings and fuselage, the two big main engines at the rear, and electronics equipment for the radar with an antenna mounted in the nose.

dash to enemy airspace. It can then revert to a forward swept position to sneak in at low altitude without being detected on radar. Radar can usually "see" only in straight lines. Buildings, trees, and hills help conceal the fighter coming in to attack. In this way, one simple design solution can turn a single aircraft into a multi-purpose weapon platform carrying out several different jobs at different times. A Russian fighter, the Su-24 Fencer, is an example of this.

Potential threats like the Russian Fencer would be met by heavyweight air superiority fighters like the twin-engined U.S. Air Force F-15 or the lightweight, single-engined F-16. The F-15 Eagle is built for rugged, all-weather tasks and has powerful armament. The F-16 Fighting Falcon is smaller, more maneuverable, and is built for close-in dog fighting. Their designs reflect the different operational roles each fighter is called upon to perform. The F-15 weighs almost twice as much as the F-16, but it can fly faster, higher, and farther. With a heavy load of weapons, the F-15 has a combat range of more than 2,500 miles. The F-16 is much more maneuverable but has a combat radius (the distance at which it can fight and still have fuel to get back) of less than 400 miles.

Rapid maneuvering at high speed causes stress measured in "g" forces. This is an

The McDonnell Douglas production line seen here is preparing F-15 Eagles for the Air Force.

Lightweight, highly agile, fighters like these F-16s built by General Dynamics stand ready at a U.S. Air Base.

apparent increase in weight for a given acceleration. For instance, if a plane makes a tight turn and pulls 3g, the plane and everything inside it weighs three times its own mass. A healthy person should be able to withstand 3g but it would be difficult to breathe and shift around in the seat. A modern high performance fighter like the F-16 can pull more than 9g in a tight turn. Although pilots get used to this with practice, the airframe must be made strong to prevent it failing under these enormous loads.

With a need for reliability and quick turnaround, fighters are built to survive conditions no other plane would fly in and yet be easy to maintain and service. The period between landing at the end of one mission, or sortie, and taking off for another is called turnaround. Quick turnaround is vital. Engines must be changed in no more than twenty minutes, airframes serviced in ten minutes, and new weapons loaded in five minutes. A modern combat fighter can get back in the air to fight again in less than thirty minutes. To make this possible, the aircraft is designed so that all engines, electronic systems, and weapons are easily accessible for ground crews.

The choice of engine, and whether to put in one engine or two, is very important. Almost all high-performance combat fighters today use an *augmented turbofan engine.* The word "augmented" means that after the engine burns the fuel in air, which has been taken in at the front and compressed by a fan, it ignites it again, giving additional thrust as the air escapes out the back. This is like an afterburner on a *turbojet engine.* Augmented turbofans have replaced afterburning turbojets because they perform better at a wide range of speeds and burn less fuel.

With engines at full thrust and after-burners lit, this F-15 climbs rapidly after a speedy take-off.

The Fighter's Teeth

Fighters are sometimes called weapon platforms because they carry large numbers of guns and rockets controlled by computers and special sensors. Before fast jets came to dominate air warfare, fighter pilots aimed their planes at an approaching enemy and fired machine guns or cannon to shoot him down. Today radar shows the pilot where the enemy is, computers help him select the weapons to use, and guidance systems control the missiles launched by the fighter plane to shoot down the hostile aircraft. All this is made possible by literally designing the fighter plane around the pilot, the engine, and the weapons it will carry. Most United States fighters use a single gun for close-in combat. Developed in the early 1960s, the General Electric M61 is both effective and reliable. Before jet fighters came along in the 1950s, the machine guns fighter pilots had to rely on were little different from those developed in the First

As two Phantoms bank hard to the right they display an assortment of underwing stores comprising air-to-air missiles, fuel tanks, and a cannon situated under the nose.

This Phantom carries a varied assortment of guided bombs, sensors and tanks.

The most common air-to-air missile in use in the Air Force today is the AIM9 Sidewinder, an infrared missile which homes on the hot exhaust of jet engines.

World War (1914-1918). Then, in the first major breakthrough for air armament, the General Electric company went back to principles first used in the famous Gatling Gun of the Old West a century ago. By packaging a cluster of six barrels around a rotating feed chamber, called the breech, a weapon of truly awesome firepower emerged.

The effectiveness of a cannon is related to the number of rounds fired each second and the weight of the projectiles fired. Each round of M61 amunition weighs about 0.77 lb. Because the gun fires up to 100 rounds per second, it is capable of putting out more than 300 lb of cannon fire in a four-second burst. A typical Russian fighter like the Mig 27 fires projectiles weighing 0.4 lb at 85 rounds per second. In a similar four-second burst it would deliver only 136 lb of firepower, less than half the weight of an M61 burst.

This F-15 Eagle carries two Sidewinder missiles close to its wing and two Sparrow on pylons below the fuselage.

This is extremely important. As it twists and turns to escape, a fighter cannot keep aim on its prey for more than a few seconds. Rate of fire and firepower is vital if the maximum amount of projectile weight is to hit the target. The M61 is installed in more United States fighters than any other gun, with provision for between 500 and 900 rounds, depending on the aircraft. One aircraft, the F-111, has provision for more than 2,000 rounds, although that number is rarely used. The plane is now mostly used for ground attack roles.

When jet fighters were first introduced in the 1950s, many people soon began to think missiles would replace guns. This has not been the case. In fact, the U.S. Air Force has only two types of air-to-air missile in common use, although fighters carry several combinations for most missions. Missiles have the advantage over guns in that they can be fired at targets not directly ahead of the attacking plane. Moreover, they can be left to reach their targets unaided while the fighter takes evasive action and escapes. Best of all, unlike any existing gun, they can hit planes a long way off.

With a range of around 11 miles, the AIM-9 Sidewinder is guided to its target by an infra-red device which homes on hot exhaust plumes. But the AIM-9 Sidewinder has limitations, because fighters can evade being hit. The AIM-7 Sparrow tracks a radar beam put out by the fighter that launched it and flies straight to the target, maneuvering to follow its twists and turns. The latest missile, the AIM-120A, has a radar seeker in its nose and follows its own tracking path, freeing the launching plane to attack other targets or escape attacks on itself. This missile began to enter service in 1987 and will eventually replace most versions of Sparrow and Sidewinder.

This AIM-7 Sparrow has just been released from an F-15 Eagle and is seen streaking to its target.

The Fighter in Combat

The cockpit of this F-16 Falcon is laid out to give the pilot easy reach to any of the instruments and controls. Note the side-stick controller and the ejection seat handle between the pilot's legs.

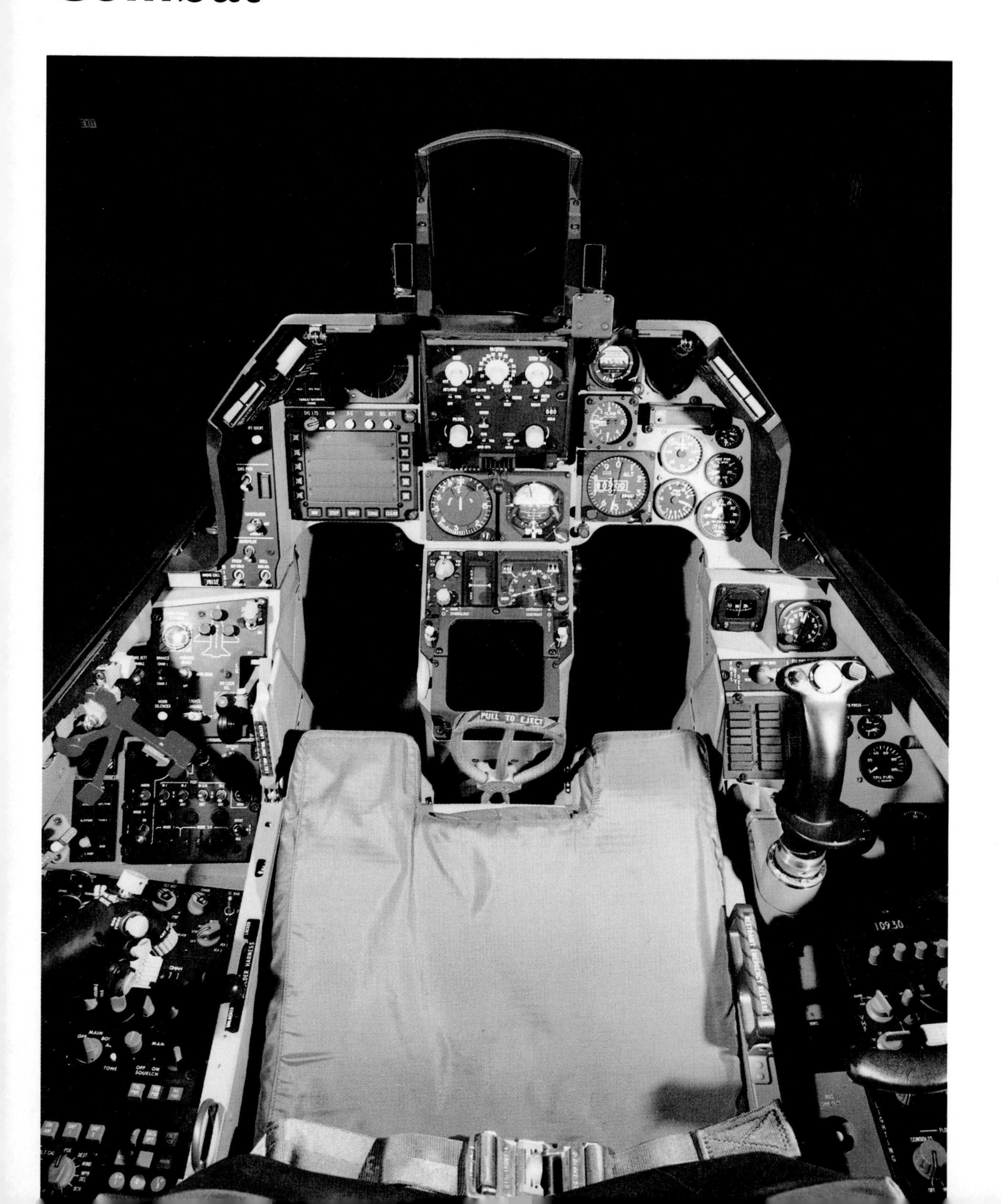

Fighters like the F-16 are built for agility, quick maneuvering, and the ability to climb high and fast.

Because the pilot and his machine must operate as a single unit, a manned fighter plane is called a total weapon system. This means that the human skills of the pilot are used to maximum effect by special computers and electronically driven controls. For instance, automatic control systems provide the pilot with an alternate set of programs, much as a computer can use different pieces of software. For example, in the F-16 the pilot can flick a switch to select ground attack electronics or, by another flick of the same switch, move to an air combat program. By doing this, he instructs the aircraft to set up the correct attack commands linking the appropriate weapons.

To perform efficiently, a fighter plane must be very agile and capable of extraordinary maneuvers. No other military aircraft in the sky today is designed to fly quite like a fighter, although the needs and capabilities of various fighters differ according to their roles. Some fighters are built for the air-superiority role and must range over long distances at great speed to intercept light bombers and strike planes that would threaten home bases. Even with fast turn-around times, most aircraft spend the majority of their time on the ground getting ready for a mission. If the enemy wants to disable an air force, it is wise to knock out the airfields rather than pick off individual planes in the sky. This is why an attacking force of fighter-bombers must be held back and destroyed close to their own airspace.

Air-interception calls for rugged planes capable of flying low and fast to escape detection from radar scanners on the attacking fighter-bombers. Then they must move swiftly to knock down these planes in combat maneuvers that put great stress on man and machine. Ability to avoid detection is important, because it enables the fighters to gain advantage. No fighter pilot wants to be seen before he first gets

The pilot gets only seconds to lock on his target and release missiles that allow the plane to break off the engagement and escape.

his sights on the enemy. For that reason a successful encounter sometimes means taking longer over the approach phase to sneak in unobserved. Only then can he get a solid lock on the attacking bomber, who also is probably trying to sneak in without being seen, and fire his missiles.

Fighters are made agile primarily to escape attack or to hold on to an enemy plane trying to get away. That same agility comes in very useful when a wise fighter pilot tries to maneuver in such a manner that his opponent never sees him coming in the first place. By far the majority of successful "kills" are made in this way. Nobody wants to be a hero unnecessarily, and every fighter pilot wants to avoid a dog-fight that might bring about his own end. There is a saying in the Air Force that there are old pilots, and there are bold pilots, but no pilots that are both old and bold!

One form of defense that probably needs more dog-fighting than any other is the air-combat role. Unlike long-range interception, where defending fighters travel long distances to stop the enemy, air combat means getting up quickly at short notice and attacking enemy planes that have penetrated the outer defenses. In some situations, gaining control of the skies can require major air battles involving many planes. Everyone is on the lookout, and there are few places to hide. Situations like these call for all the skill and expertise a pilot can summon to stay alive, let alone bring down attacking planes. It is here that strong nerves, cool discipline, and a very good knowledge of the aircraft keeps the fighter pilot on top.

When and where to attack is very important because a pilot gets only a few seconds to lock his electronic sights on the target and fire. When his limited supply of missiles is gone, high-velocity guns are the only weapons left. To use them, the pilot must get in even closer, further reducing the time the target stays in sight. Only through constant practice in peacetime can a fighter pilot stay in shape for the ultimate test in battle-filled skies.

Opposite, top:* *No fighter pilot ever hopes his enemy will get a view like this. Hidden from view, he would be in a prime position to attack.

Opposite, bottom:* *An F-15 conducts a close inspection escort of a Russian bomber on a reconnaissance mission.

Attack

Not all fighters play a defensive role. Some are designed to attack and help stop enemy forces before they gain control of ground or air space. Once called fighter-bombers, ground attack air craft are now called *strike* or *interdiction* planes. They are derived from heavy air-superiority fighters. Some are capable of delivering comparatively large bomb loads over short distances. These are termed multi-role combat planes. One example is the F-16, capable of carrying 10,000 lb of bombs and air-to-ground rockets, called stores, on a full load of fuel or

Built from a design that lost out to the F-16, this F-18 navy plane has been bought by several countries as a land-based attack fighter. It is known as the CF-18.

15,000 lb with less fuel. In either case, strike range is just a few hundred miles.

Another plane, the CF-18, was converted from a U.S. Navy fighter called the F/A-18 Hornet into a land-based attack fighter. The CF-18 is technically capable of lifting 17,000 lb of stores. In practice, it carries much less, and a typical load would consist of ten 500 lb bombs, nine 1,000 lb bombs, and additional underwing fuel tanks. With a stores weight of this size, the plane has a range of more than 400 miles. It is primarily as a multi-role fighter that the CF-18 sees most use, however, combining both light ground attack and air superiority roles.

Biggest of the group in the all-weather strike role is the General Dynamics F-111. First flown in December, 1964, this swing-wing design is built to fly very fast, very close to the ground. With two big augmented turbofan engines, the F-111 has a top speed of *Mach 2.2* (more than twice the speed of sound), or 1,450 MPH. This plane can carry bombs in a special internal bay and a wide range of external stores on pylons that pivot as the wings sweep forward or back. This keeps the pylons and their stores facing forward at all times. Some versions of the F-111 weigh up to 100,000 lb carrying a maximum weapon load of about 24,000 lb. Most have a range of between 1,000 miles and 3,200 miles.

The swing-wing F-111 has seen considerable service as an all-weather strike plane and in that role is currently used by the Air Force as a Mach 2 fighter-bomber capable of carrying up to 24,000 lbs of bombs.

Adapted from the F-15 Eagle, versions like this have proven capable of carrying heavy weights across long distances to strike at targets deep behind enemy lines.

The ultimate development of the basic F-111 has given it the job of delivering Short Range Attack Missiles, called SRAM, or the Air Launched Cruise Missile. These are called *stand-off weapons* because they are released from an aircraft which is said to be "stood off" from the target. They fly on their own using special radar systems to guide them to within a hundred few yards of their targets. As soon as they are released, the plane is free to return home alone. The SRAM can fly up to 100 miles, ducking and weaving to escape enemy defenses on a special programmed course. Cruise missiles can be instructed to fly any programmed pattern to a maximum distance of 1,500 miles.

Some planes start life as air superiority fighters and because of modifications grow into strike planes. Such is the case with the McDonnell Douglas F-15E, developed as an all-weather interceptor. This plane is to enter service with the U.S. Air Force in the late 1980s to help expand the ground attack mission flown by F-111s. The F-15E will carry about the same load as an F-111 and fly almost as far. It is faster, capable of reaching Mach 2.5, or 1,653 MPH and is better in combat.

The F-15E is fitted with advanced engines more powerful than those in the F-111 and is very good in the air superiority role. It can fly 40 percent farther than other F-15s because it has special fuel tanks. These are called *conformal tanks* because they are shaped to fit underneath the plane and are, therefore, said to "conform" with its general outline. With conformal tanks and a full load of weapons, the F-15E can play the role of a strike plane. With bombs gone and more than half the fuel used up, it converts into a maneuverable dog-fighter to fight itself out of a scrap.

Releasing its load of bombs on a tactical target, the F-15 converts to a very able fighter plane.

The lightweight F-16 fighter drops a GBU-10 laser-guided bomb from an altitude of 5,000 feet before the pilot rapidly makes an evasive turn after separation.

The Balance of Power

United States fighter planes exist to protect the United States from attack by enemy bombers and other intruders. They also exist to support the air forces of our allies against aggression. The United States is a founding member of NATO, the North Atlantic Treaty Organization. Formed in 1949, less than four years after the end of the Second World War (1939-45), NATO also includes membership of Canada, Iceland, Great Britain, and eleven other European countries. It is based on the principle that an attack on one is an attack on all. In other words, if any NATO member country is attacked, all the others will go to its aid.

U.S. Air Force fighters are operated by one of four commands: Tactical Air Command (TAC), United States Air Forces in Europe (USAFE), Pacific Air Forces (PAF), and the Alaskan Air Command (AAC). Tactical Air Command is responsible for the defense of the continental United States, known in military circles as CONUS. The other three commands serve in Europe, on the Pacific bases, and in Alaska. The U.S. Air Force has about half its people and equipment overseas, which means that TAC is as big as the other three fighter commands together.

The Soviet Union poses the biggest military challenge to the United States, because it has by far the largest armed forces outside NATO. In 1955 the Soviet Union formed a military alliance, called the Warsaw Pact, with Bulgaria, Czechoslovakia, East Germany, Hungary, Poland, and Rumania. All these countries were overrun by

In support of NATO, Air Force fighters must operate in places as remote as Alaska and the cloudy and often rain-soaked countryside of Northern Europe.

Ever ready against surprise attack on these frontiers, fighter pilots get regular briefings for routine missions.

Russia at the end of the Second World War, and communist governments were set up. It is in Europe, therefore, that democratic NATO countries face a potential threat from the combined forces of the Warsaw Pact.

Fighter pilots are on constant standby in case of readiness, but at other times can frequently be found flying training missions.

Regular flying and constant practice keeps both men and machines in a state of preparedness and training even extends to the simulated use of live bombs.

The U.S. Air Force has about 700 fighters, interceptors and ground attack planes in Europe. Altogether, the other NATO countries have more than 2,000 planes like these, for a total of nearly 2,800 NATO planes. Against this, the Warsaw Pact countries have nearly 5,000, almost twice as many. These totals include all the different categories of fighter, strike and interdiction planes. The biggest imbalance is in the pure fighter and interceptor forces. NATO has just over 500 compared with more than 2,400 from the Warsaw Pact.

Fighters, interceptors, and attack planes account for about one-third of all the aircraft in the U.S. Air Force. The average air force squadron has between 18 and 24 fighters or attack planes, compared with between 11 and 17 for bomber squadrons. The air forces differ in the exact number of aircraft in each squadron but most are in a similar range.

For a long time, NATO has relied on the quality of its planes and their pilots to balance overwhelming superiority in numbers from Russia and her allies. For more than forty years, the United States and other non-communist countries have spent much less on defense than Warsaw Pact countries. Now, with increasing use of modern technology, Soviet fighter planes are becoming a real match for NATO pilots. Performance is better than ever before and modernization of Russia's immense armed forces provides the Soviet Union with a powerful military might.

Politicians decide how much money will be spent on defense in the United States. Military planners advise the politicians on which weapons are needed most. Fighters and attack planes are important because they support ground forces and help destroy enemy strike planes. Because fighter planes are expensive and it also costs a lot to train pilots, the quality of their equipment is vital. Even though NATO policy is to rely on quality rather than quantity, there is need for a strong fighter force at home and abroad.

On some long duration missions in support of alliance obligations to NATO, fighters will frequently have to refuel in the air from special tanker planes.

Threats to the Fighter

Soviet early-warning planes fly regular patrol over territory close to NATO countries and here an escorting Soviet fighter is seen on its reconnaissance mission.

Fighters are valuable weapons in any defense force. They help protect defending planes responding to surprise attack, patrol the skies for enemy planes, and pose a continual threat to aggressive air forces. It is not surprising that a great deal of money and effort has gone into the problem of knocking fighters and attack planes out of the sky. Unlike big bombers that strike targets deep inside enemy airspace, fighters both guard friendly forces and pose an awesome threat to the enemy.

The Soviet Union has the largest array of air defense weapons ever put together. Until the early 1980s, most Soviet attack planes were inferior to those of the United States and NATO. They did not have the same performance and

One of the most lethal Soviet fighters in the sky today is the Mig-29 Fulcrum, several of which are seen here in formation.

they were not as reliable. Great improvements in maintaining NATO fighters helped keep this lead. Better reliability helped increase the number of missions a NATO fighter could fly each day. With less time on the ground there was more time in the air, where a fighter earns its keep.

In the early 1970s, the Soviet Air Force began to use long range bombers that could threaten the United States. These were called Backfire. By the early 1990s the Russians will introduce the Blackjack to widespread service. The Blackjack has even greater range and can carry a full warload more than 4,500 miles. It is capable of flying at twice the speed of sound. To protect these bombers and other shorter range attack planes, the Mig-29 Fulcrum has been put into service.

The Mig-29 is an interceptor with great maneuverability, and its weapon system, consisting of radar to pick out targets and missiles to fire at them, is able to attack very low-flying aircraft. Picking out low-flying aircraft is difficult, because radar can be very easily confused with reflections from rock, buildings, or any solid substance on the ground. It is even more difficult to build a missile that can keep track of a low-flying target and hit it. The ability to sneak in without being seen is one reason that modern attack planes fly very close to the ground. The new Russian interceptors have radar that can point down to the ground and pick up low-flying planes, and they have missiles that can go after them. Because of these features, the new weapon system is said to give the interceptor a *look-down/shoot-down* capability.

Another look-down/shoot-down fighter is the Sukhoi Su-27 Flanker, with a range of more than 900 miles carrying six air-to-air missiles. Most daunting of all, however, is the new Mig-31 Foxhound. Able to fly at Mach 2.4, it is comparable to the McDonnell Douglas F-15. Foxhound can carry up to eight air-to-air missiles and has a reported range of 1,300 miles. It is highly maneuverable and handles well. None of these planes could reach the United States, fight a battle, and return to Soviet bases. They could, however, threaten United States and NATO forces in Europe, the Pacific, and Alaska.

The Soviet Union has the largest force of surface-to-air missiles (called SAMs) in the

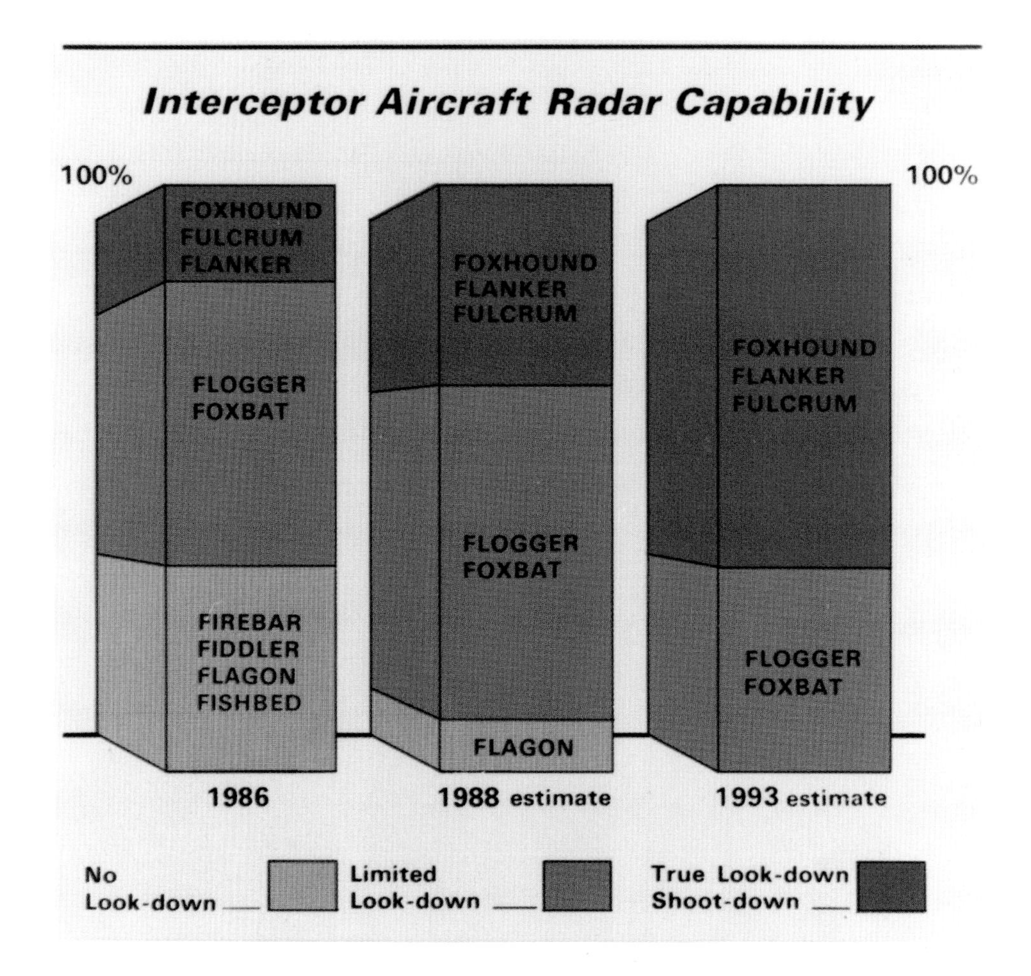

Known as look-down/shoot-down, interceptor radars that can attack planes flying very close to the ground have enormous capability over low-flying intruders. This shows how the development of such radars is extending to the complete range of Soviet fighters recorded here by their NATO code-names such as Foxhound, Flogger and Firebar.

The Mig-29 has full look-down/shoot-down capability and is here seen on patrol photographed from a NATO fighter.

world. They have about 13,600 SAM launchers and 10,000 radar units. SAMs are fired from the ground to pre-set heights, homing on aircraft picked up by radar. They are the biggest single threat to interceptors and strike planes. Soviet radar units cover the sky from low to high altitude, watching far beyond the Soviet border. They are equipped to control some of the most powerful SAMs ever built.

Some of these can hit planes 30 miles away, flying high and fast, while others are built to hit low-flying planes coming in over the tree-tops. Recently, a formidable range of new SAMs has been deployed. Most of these new weapons are highly mobile and can move from place to place very quickly. Hidden in woods or clearings, they are difficult to detect and pose a serious threat to any patrolling fighter flying by.

For planes that get through the low-flying interceptors, the surface-to-air missile is a constant threat to fighter planes attacking inside enemy air space. These Soviet SAMs are typical of the several thousand used throughout the Soviet Union.

The Pilots

Some people say that fighter pilots are not made, they are born. What they mean is that the really good fighter pilots have a natural talent in them that no amount of training could put there. That may be so, but without rigorous training, natural skills never develop properly, and the best talents remain hidden.

Fighter pilots today are skilled people who must know a lot about their planes. They must understand the way the plane is designed and the mechanics of its operation. Fighter pilots and their planes are a total weapon system, operating as team players with many different elements involved. Each pilot must come to feel a living part of his machine and to understand the ways it will react to aggressive, sometimes violent, handling. The speed at which air battles are fought means there is little time to plan strategy in the middle of a dog-fight. A cool head and tight discipline leads to self-control, putting the pilot totally on top of the situation. Only with these self-imposed standards will he live to fight another day. Experience and the combined use of talent, training, and knowledge goes into every surviving fighter pilot.

Fighter pilots spend a lot of time getting to know their planes because it is there that the greatest threat to their life will occur and they must know every part of its instrumentation and performance.

Simulators driven by computers like this shown here give fighter pilots realistic situations where they can practice various combat maneuvers that in real life might end in an accident. It is here that they learn how to perfect the best maneuvers for all kinds of combat situations.

Pilots begin by learning to fly. They then apply for a place at fighter school. They must pass rigorous tests and examinations. Assessing their characters and personalities becomes an important part of the selection process. If successful, they will be called upon to work with a team of people. Some of these will be their own colleagues, with whom they must coordinate operations in the air or fight with to protect airspace. Understanding the personalities of their colleagues is an important part of knowing how they will respond to emergency situations.

Other people with whom fighter pilots must work are the ground crews who service the aircraft and their engines. These people maintain the planes in top condition. Pilots must develop a

Pilots must know their planes well and get along well with ground crew whose job it is to keep the machines in top condition under any circumstances, day or night.

Trainee pilots graduate to simulated combat exercises with real planes in mock battle.

strong and confident relationship with them, so that both ground crews and pilots trust each other's judgment. Each must learn to work with the other. Another group within the team are the flight controllers, who track enemy planes and keep the fighters informed of target positions.

Only when the trainee pilots pass all these conditions and show a ready willingness to cooperate and work in a team will they be trusted with expensive fighter planes. At first they fly special trainers built to help good pilots become better. They will learn about complex maneuvers and test their own flying skills with more advanced equipment. They will be taught the principles of high-speed flying and how they can get the ultimate performance from their planes.

Then they will graduate to operational combat fighters and be assigned a unit where their own performance will be assessed. Because a vital ingredient in every good fighter pilot is experience, continual practice is essential. This helps make a good pilot a safe pilot, another asset at squadron level. When working as part of a team of pilots in the sky, safety is as important as the performance of the plane. Highly skilled pilots are put to the test at air force Red Flag exercises. In these, planes that simulate Russian fighters are put up against standard U.S. Air Force interceptors so both sides can learn how to perform the best and most effective combat maneuvers. Real battles are flown, with no live bullets or missiles.

The ultimate reward for excellence is to graduate to a test pilot school where pilots learn how to check out new fighters. This job calls for sound engineering knowledge, and from there, there is only one place to go for the bright, successful test pilot — into space as an astronaut.

Head-on engagements like this are a common occurrence in realistic combat maneuvers to test the agility of the plane and the reaction time of the pilot.

Training Planes

Nobody ejects from an airplane just for fun but fighter pilots do sometimes have to get out of their aircraft quickly during an emergency. Here a test pilot is seen evaluating a new ejection seat.

The most successful and widely used trainer in the Air Force is the Northrop T-38 Talon.

Fighter pilots need good and reliable equipment for training. Training aids like simulators can teach them only so much. Very sophisticated devices can help put realistic situations up on a screen as a pilot sits in a cockpit mock-up "flying" a simulator. However, the only way to get a realistic feel for combat flying is to do it in the air. Training planes are an essential element in the fighter pilot's course, beginning when they first learn to fly.

Good training planes provide a wide range of opportunities, taking the student from basic flying to advanced *aerobatics*. One plane in particular has served the U.S. Air Force well for 25 years. Built by Northrop, it is the T-38 Talon. Back in the mid-1950s, Northrop designed a low-cost fighter for sale to developing nations. It had a small airframe, two reliable turbojet engines with afterburners to carry it through the speed of sound, and pylons under the wings for weapons in addition to four guns.

Before this plane, called the F-5 Freedom Fighter, could be developed as a lightweight fighter, it was adapted as the T-38 Talon trainer, which entered service in 1961. The fighter version's first flight was two years later, in 1963, and was the beginning of a long and successful career.

In all, more than 2,600 F-5 fighters were built in the United States and abroad, used in 31 countries, and developed into twenty different versions. A special trainer version, the F-5B was designed for fighter pilots. In this way, Northrop provided a package of tactical fighter, ground attack, and reconnaissance planes (variants of the F-5A) with the two-seater (F-5B) to train pilots for the combat models.

The U.S. Air Force uses the F-5 as "aggressor" planes in the development of combat tactics

The Talon was developed from a lightweight fighter called the F-5 which has been used in many countries around the world as a low-cost interceptor.

Good pilots go on to be members of aerobatic team like the Thunderbirds shown here flying their newly-acquired F-16s.

during advanced training games. With highly experienced pilots flying standard F-15 or F-16 fighters, "aggressors" in F-5s play the role of enemy pilots in high speed dog-fights. Aggressor squadrons operate in the United States, England, and the Philippines. The U.S. Navy uses aggressor units at Miramar Naval Air Station, California, and Oceana Naval Air Station, Virginia.

While the F-5 has largely been exported overseas as a low-cost fighter, the T-38 Talon has stayed at home. Serving to train air force and navy pilots, a few Talons have been sold to NASA for the personal use of astronauts. The T-38 has been an outstandingly successful trainer, with 1,187 built before production ended in 1972. In all its years of service, the T-38 Talon has accumulated more than 9 million flying hours and is adding to that total by more than 400,000 flight hours each year.

The T-38 has a maximum speed of Mach 1.3, or 858 mph at a height of 36,000 feet, and it has a range of 1,140 miles. Yet it weighs only 7,164 pounds empty and has a maximum takeoff weight of less than 12,000 pounds. A modern combat fighter can weigh anywhere between 24,000 pounds and 90,000 pounds. Despite its light weight, it is a safe trainer to fly. Against an expected loss rate of 12 planes for every 100,000 flying hours, the U.S. Air force has actually lost less than two. The T-38 was the first supersonic aircraft in the United States to complete its first 2,000 flights without a major accident. For eight years the Talon served as the aircraft flown by the air force flight demonstration team, the Thunderbirds. It has also established four international time-to-climb records achieved by reaching certain altitudes in the shortest time from takeoff. Famous pilot Jacqueline Cochrane has set eight women's flying records in this plane.

The T-38 is destined to be the longest-serving trainer, perhaps the longest-serving plane, in the U.S. Air Force inventory. Northrop is manufacturing new wings for the Talon family that should see the plane through to the year 2010. If that happens, it will have served the U.S. Air Force for fifty years!

Trainer planes are sometimes so successful that they find service in many different roles, as with this F-5 adapted as a light strike plane.

Supporting the Fighters

Chosen for its long range and high performance the KC-10A Extender is now being used by the Air Force as an aerial tanker and logistics plane to ferry fighters overseas when needed during emergency.

Fighters are sometimes used to help defend the territory of our allies overseas. To support these aircraft that have been ferried overseas by air, a large amount of equipment must be flown to the region. During one such operation to support Israel, some countries refused to allow air force cargo planes and tankers to land on their territory. This refusal seriously hampered U.S. operations. This was in 1973, and within a year the U.S. Air Force came up with plans for an Advanced Tanker/Cargo Aircraft (AT/CA) that could help lift supplies directly to the war zone.

The plane chosen to meet this requirement was a modified version of the McDonnell Douglas DC-10 airliner. Called the KC-10A Extender, it could serve either as an aerial tanker or as a logistics plane delivering large loads of cargo across great distances. For the tanker role, seven separate fuel compartments are installed below the main deck usually used for cargo. The compartments are connected together and have a maximum capacity of nearly 118,000 pounds of fuel in addition to the plane's existing supply of 238,000 pounds. Refueling fighters in the air is possible with a special probe capable of moving 1,500 gallons a minute.

Altogether, the KC-10A Extender can hold more than 51,000 gallons of fuel. This fuel can be used either for refueling operations or for giving the plane extra range. Because the added fuel compartments are below the cargo deck, normal storage space is not affected. This combination makes the Extender an ideal plane for helping

ferry fighter units, their equipment, personnel, and supplies. In one typical mission, F-16 or F-15 fighters accompanying the cargo-tanker could top-up their fuel tanks from a single Extender, stretching their range and providing a single flight from the United States to their destination. The U.S. Air Force plans to buy a total of 60 KC-10As to use with other big transport planes when needs arise.

Although about half the U.S. Air Force's tactical fighter force is based in the United States,

Other planes like this KC-135 tanker are used to ferry fighters from the United States to bases overseas.

This F-15 takes on fuel from a tanker as it prepares for a long flight across the Atlantic Ocean.

In support of a major military operation in some far off country, ground support equipment will follow the rapid deployment of fighters.

it could be rapidly deployed to foreign bases in the event of war. The fighters could ferry themselves across the Atlantic or the Pacific Ocean, refueling as they went. All the stores and supplies, however, would require a major airlift using all sorts of heavy transport planes. Biggest of all is the Lockheed C-5 Galaxy. Weighing up to 769,000 pounds, it has a maximum range of nearly 6,900 miles. With a wing span of more than 222 feet and a length of almost 248 feet, the Galaxy is one of the world's biggest aircraft.

During the late 1970s, in response to several military operations from the Soviet Union, particularly the invasion of Afghanistan, President Carter greatly improved the Rapid Deployment Force, or RDF. This is not a specific unit or military command but rather a group of land, sea, and air forces from the army, the navy and the air force. Put together for a particular job, the RDF is designed to deploy a wide range of weapons to a trouble spot anywhere in the world quickly and efficiently.

The need to move men and material quickly from one place to another greatly improved mobility during the 1980s. Today, United States forces are better equipped than ever before to respond rapidly and with force to protect life and property overseas. Any major war fought by the United States would require massive airlift on a huge scale. To carry large numbers of men and their equipment, and to help ferry the fighters across, the U.S. Air Force has more than 1,000 transport planes. Some are quite small but nearly 400 are the size of the Galaxy and the Extender.

The most responsible job for this force is to move so quickly that conflict is avoided or to stop conflict quickly when it breaks out. The best and most effective fighter is the one that never fires its guns in anger.

Typical of places where U.S. Air Force fighters have to operate, this spectacular view of the pyramids is seen as F-16 Falcons fly over Cairo in Egypt.

HL
388
HL
385
HL
107
HL
AF 79 386

ABBREVIATIONS

AAC	Alaskan Air Command
AT/CA	Advanced Tanker/Cargo Aircraft
CONUS	Continental United States
NATO	North Atlantic Treaty Organization
PAF	Pacific Air Force
RDF	Rapid Deployment Force
SAM	Surface-To-Air Missile
SRAM	Short Range Attack Missile
TAC	Tactical Air Command
USAF	United States Air Force
USAFE	United States Air Forces in Europe

GLOSSARY

Aerobatics	Spectacular maneuvers or stunts performed by an airplane, usually involving rolls, loops, and snap-turns.
Augmented turbofan engine	A jet engine with circular compressors to increase the volume of air taken in through the front, with burners behind the combustion chamber to give additional energy to the exhausted gases by reigniting them as they leave the nozzle.
Conformal tanks	Fuel tanks shaped to follow the outline of the airplane, providing minimum air resistance. In effect, conformal tanks are a modeled addition to the airplane itself rather than obviously attached structures.
Interdiction planes	Fighter or fighter-bomber planes designed to project force to an enemy offensively rather than react defensively to enemy attack.
Mach	Mach 1, or unity, is the speed of sound: 760 MPH at sea level, decreasing to 660 MPH at a height of 36,000 feet. Mach 2.2 is equivalent to a speed of 1672 MPH at sea level or 1,452 MPH above 36,000 feet.
Look-down/shoot-down shoot-down	The capability for a radar to spot extremely low-flying targets, such as strike planes, and then control missiles firing to intercept and destroy them.
Sortie	One of several types of missions, such as striking the enemy or conducting a reconnaissance, that begins with take off and ends with landing.
Stand off weapons	Bombs and rockets with a form of rocket or turbojet propulsion that enables them to fly several hundred miles to a target behind enemy lines.
Strike planes	Interdiction planes that carry bombs dropped on land targets.
Supersonic	Speeds higher than the speed of sound, which is about 760 MPH at sea level, slowly decreasing to about 660 MPH at an altitude of 36,000 feet and above.
Total weapon system	The combination of airplane and pilot, when equipped as a weapon platform in an attacking situation.
Turbojet engine	A pure jet engine that re-ignites the burnt fuel-air mixture but without compressor blades in front.
Variable-geometry	A means by which the shape of an airplane wing can be changed in flight by attaching the wing to a pivot where it joins the main body (fuselage) so it can be swiveled to any position. This wing design is also called the swing-wing.
Weapon platform	A term used to describe an airplane that carries guns, rockets, bombs, and missiles to a position where they can strike the enemy.

INDEX

Page references in *italics* indicate photographs or illustrations.